THE ULTIMATE BOOK OF FARTING

There must be an angel
Playing with my fart

ST. PETER

If I am in a restaurant and I'm eating and someone says, 'Hey, do you mind if I smoke?' I always say, 'No, do you mind if I fart?'

STEVE MARTIN

Oi loikes cheese 'cos cheese makes I fart, and when I farts I knows is'e helffy.

SENT IN BY FRANK BAKER WHO HAS BEEN
GIGGLING ABOUT THIS ADVICE GIVEN TO
HIM BY AN OLD CHAP ON A FARM ON
HOLIDAY 30 YEARS AGO

I have more talent in my smallest fart than you have in your entire body.

WALTER MATTHAU TO BARBRA STREISAND

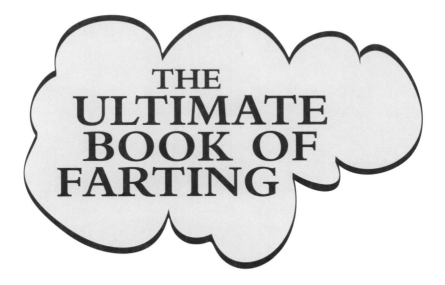

THE ULTIMATE BOOK OF FARTING

BY
ALEC BROMCIE

Michael O'Mara Humour

First published in Great Britain in 2000 by
Michael O'Mara Books Limited
9 Lion Yard
Tremadoc Road
London SW4 7NQ

Some of the material in this book was originally published in *The Complete Book of Farting* © 1999 Michael O'Mara Books

A CIP catalogue record for this book is available from the British Library

ISBN 1-85479-582-1

3 5 7 9 10 8 6 4 2

Original concept and compilation by David Crombie
Designed and typeset by Design 23
Printed and bound in China by Leo Paper Products

www.mombooks.com

ABOUT THE AUTHOR

Alec Bromcie is Visiting Professor of Wind and Sound at the University of Valparaíso. He is the author of many academic papers and theses on the subject of farting and has decided to publish his latest ideas and research findings in this book. His *The Little Book of Farting* was a bestseller in 1999 and was translated into various languages. Because of this, he has been much in demand on the lecture circuit and has given a speech to the UN about the effects of flatulence on global warming.

He is currently single, has three children, two pet skunks and lives in Pratts Bottom, England.

He can be contacted at
alec.bromcie@michaelomarabooks.com

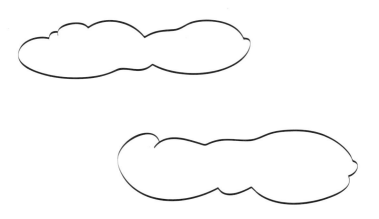

PUBLISHER'S DISCLAIMER

A cautionary note from one of our readers:

> *Dear Professor Bromcie*
> *A copy of your book,* The Complete Book of Farting, *was given to me for Christmas and I found it so funny I had to read some of it aloud. Now my mother-in-law has promised never to come here again. How can I repay you?*
> STEVE

CONTENTS

ACKNOWLEDGEMENTS

Since the publication last year of *The Little Book of Farting*, I have been overwhelmed by the number of letters and e-mails from readers of the book. I would like to take this opportunity to thank all of them for their comments and stories, some of which are included in this book. As always, the editorial staff at Michael O'Mara excelled themselves and special thanks must go to Jacquie Wind, Helen Blowers and Bryony Bubbles. Creating the sound chip was a labour of love by David Brann and we must thank Martin and Yvette for spending time and effort recording farts over a period of three months. These were digitally processed and the results were shortened to the four you hear in this book. Never has so much wind been passed by so few for so many! Their perseverance and dedication will never be forgotten. I would also like to thank my ancestor, Baron Phillipe de Bromcey, who came over with William the Conqueror almost a thousand years ago. It was because of him that the family got its coat of arms and the motto 'Veni, Vidi, Inflatiavi' ('I came, I saw, I gassed them'). Lastly, a big thank you to Caroline, Kate, Suzanne and Eliza, who kept me smiling when the atmosphere in the research laboratory was hanging like a cloud over my head.

A QUICK BLAST FROM THE PAST

Let's get this straight to begin with – everybody farts. FARTS ARE 100 PER CENT NORMAL! They are a vital and inescapable part of everyday life and are nothing to be prudish about. When God created man, and notably woman, he meant them to do what comes naturally, and fart away Adam and Eve no doubt did, particularly with all those fruit trees around.

The Old Testament aside, flatulence has an ancient and honourable history, at least where the medical profession is concerned. The great Hippocrates of Cos (c. 460 BC – c. 377, c. 359 or c. 357 BC; the authorities differ) made certain that doctors should understand the mechanics of farting, and they and their patients the consequences. If some of his theories have not withstood the test of time and the relentless march of medicine – hardly very surprising, given that he was practising some 2,300 years ago – he remains sound on flatulence. Of the consequences of farting, he had this to say about the avoidance of what patent–medicine advertisements call 'abdominal pain':

> *It is best to pass wind noiselessly, but even a noisy fart is better than one retained . . . Pains and swelling in the* hypochondria *[situated in the upper abdomen, and believed by the ancient Greeks to be the seat of melancholy] are much reduced by* borborygmi *[rumblings of gas in the intestines] in the* hypochondrium *[upper abdomen] . . . much relief will be effected by the gas moving along, and also by its descent to the lower bowels.*

9

Hippocrates seems, too, to have had a pretty good sense not only of the nature of farting, but also of how the human body operates:

> *The factors that cause flatulence or* tormina *['acute griping or ringing pains in the bowels' – OED; the word derives from the same root as 'torment'] . . . naturally do so in the hollow parts of the body, the stomach and chest, where they produce rumbling noises . . .*

Now we know what we're dealing with, I will move on.

DR BROMCIE'S CASEBOOK

Since the publication of *The Complete Book of Farting,* I have received lots of letters and e-mails thanking me for explaining the science and practice of farting. They have also raised many other pertinent queries and I provide below answers to the most interesting questions on farting.
Here comes the science!

WHAT IS A FART?

Farts are nature's way of releasing our own toxins. Flatulence can be described as the pressure of excessive amounts of gas in the stomach or intestines. If we didn't fart, the gases we produce would be reabsorbed into the blood and poison us. And, as anyone who has ever suffered from trapped wind can verify, holding it in causes painful swelling and distension of the abdomen. In the many years I have devoted to the subject of farting, I haven't heard of a single human being who has actually filled to bursting point – unlike cows which explode regularly. Farts are mainly composed of five gases:

Nitrogen (N_2)
Carbon dioxide (CO_2)
Hydrogen (H_2)
Methane (CH_4)
Oxygen (O_2)

WHAT'S IN A FART?

The gases listed above are OK so far as they go, but hydrogen, nitrogen and oxygen are elements and by themselves will not give the true flavour of a fart. What they need is a bit of spicing up and they get this by forming compounds with carbon (C) and sulphur (S). This is the method of creation of such essential smell-factor ingredients as skatol (C_9H_9N) which is composed of nine parts carbon, nine parts hydrogen and one part nitrogen.

Of course, each and every fart will vary, but there have to be some standards – we're talking science here, not social. To get to the fart of the matter, if you'll forgive the pun, I have listed the properties of the various components of a fart below:

Properties of Carbon Dioxide (or Carbon-acid gas):
- A heavy gas which accounts for up to 50-60% of the gas in a fart
- Formed during respiration and the combustion of organic compounds
- Dissolves in water to make carbonic acid, H_2CO_3, which is what makes drinks fizzy and, in turn, what results in those bubbles in the bath
- Does not support combustion, hence is used in fire-extinguishers (worth noting for those that must set light to their farts!)
- Also colourless so it won't be responsible for those unfortunate brown marks that can sometimes appear on men's underpants (no woman has ever admitted to this happening to her)

12

- CO_2 is heavier than air so that its presence in a smelly fart also means that the smell tends to hang around (NB. CO_2 is absorbed by plants through photosynthesis, so if you get caught out, fart under a tree)
- CO_2 is a suffocating gas but not toxic – it might finish you off if you farted in a cupboard for a few days, but you won't die from sniffing a single fart
- Can be narcotic in high quantities (i.e. CO_2 narcosis)

Properties of Nitrogen:
- Predominates in farting by the formation of compounds such as indol and skatol
- Colourless
- Odourless
- Relatively unreactive
- Forms 78% of the air we breathe

Properties of Hydrogen
- The lightest and most abundant element in the universe
- Highly flammable
- Stinks when reacted with sulphur to form the compound hydrogen sulphide
- Colourless
- Used in the formation of bombs in which energy is released by fusion of hydrogen nuclei

Properties of Methane
- Also known as natural gas or marsh gas. Methane is produced by the decomposition of organic matter, and swamps, marshes and river-beds often contain large amounts of decomposing vegetation. Since the food we eat also undergoes a process of decomposition (due to the action of *E. coli* microbes in the large bowel), and since food is almost entirely organic matter, it is not at all surprising that methane is present in farts
- Flammable: when lit will appear as a strong blue or green flame – DON'T TRY IT!
- Increased by eating beans
- Makes coal mines explode. Methane is a product of the carbonization of coal. The explosive mixture of hydrocarbons, mainly methane, found in coal mines is known as 'firedamp'; after a firedamp explosion, a poisonous mixture of gases, mostly carbon monoxide, is left; this is known as 'afterdamp', while the mixture of poisonous gases just generally found in mines – chiefly carbon monoxide – is called 'whitedamp'. It is a little known fact that miners never fart – they have enough to worry about without adding 'browndamp' to their problems

- Methane from the flatulence of cattle and sheep is said to be damaging the ozone layer
- Tarzan, who lived entirely on jungly vegetables, was greeted by his lady friend with the wrinkled-nose exclamation: 'You Tarzan! – Methane!'

Properties of Oxygen:
- Colourless, tasteless, odourless, highly reactive; essential for all aerobic respiration and almost all combustion
- Commonest element in the Earth's crust
- There are often only low levels of this gas in a fart but recycling it is essential for human life
- Found in the compound CO_2 (see above)

Methyl–indol (US: methyl–indole):
- Methyl, CH_3, is derived from methane by the removal of one hydrogen atom
- Indol, C_8H_7N, is a crystalline compound derived from decomposing proteins (i.e. grub)
- Amazingly, since its smell would curl flock wallpaper in a curry house at 100 paces, it is used in making scent

Skatol (US: skatole) – C_9H_9N

- The name, charmingly, derives from Greek *skor, skatos*, dung, from which we also derive words like scatological
- Foul-smelling
- Also in civet; hence it, too, is used in scent-making

Hydrogen Sulphide (rotten-egg gas) – H_2S

- Colourless
- Inflammable
- Soluble in water
- Poisonous
- This one's a real stinker . . .

Methyl-mercaptan

- For the methyl bit see above under Methyl-indol
- Mercaptan is any of various compounds that contain a thiol, the latter being one of several compounds analogous with alcohols, but where sulphur replaces the oxygen of the hydroxyl group

HOW DO WE FART?

The causes of tympanites are aerophagy, acute dilation of the stomach, mechanical intestinal obstruction and paralytic ileus.

THESIS ON FARTING NO. 2345 A. BROMCIE

Let's start at that very good place to begin – the beginning. Every time we open our mouths or breathe through our noses we are starting off an extraordinary chain of events. We take in air and, as we all know, what goes in must come out – about 8 metres of digestive tract later. A fart begins by swallowing air. It then travels down into the stomach where, at this stage, it will be mainly composed of atmospheric nitrogen and oxygen – i.e. not much yet has happened to it. If all is going well and our insides are in regular working order, some of the oxygen will be absorbed here. However, nitrogen is largely unabsorbable and so merrily meanders on through our intestines.

It is in the intestines that carbon dioxide, methane and hydrogen are formed. The carbon dioxide, produced by fermentation, is largely absorbed.

It is a fact of life that man (or woman) cannot fart on air alone. To make a decent fart, a loud, noisy, juicy or smelly one, he (she) needs some protein and some carbohydrate – i.e. some grub.

During the digestion of food and the sorting out of the leftovers, bacteria ferment away, attacking the remains of our latest snack and blasting the food that has not been fully digested in the small or large intestine. It is at this stage that the other gases we have mentioned are produced. What we eat is important to the volume and composition of farts. Some foods prove harder to digest than others – i.e. foods which are rich in starch or cellulose such as cabbage – and these are the ones that farters love. The much maligned baked bean, for example, is a complex carbohydrate that is just mal-digested. And the same holds true for mushrooms. Many people don't realize that mushrooms contain a sugar called raffinose, which humans can't break down. The outcome: GAS!

Now we are getting ready for it. We are on amber light. The gases are all mixing together nicely, the sphincter muscle is on standby and the gases – now called flatus – are coming down the rectum. Check that the situation is a green light one and that it's suitable to pull away and PARP! – you have a fart.

Note: Gas, of course, is not the only result of Voidance. So for those that would prefer Avoidance of certain nasty accidents - do be careful where and when you let go.

HOW OFTEN DO WE FART?

The Guinness Book Of Records holds statistics on neither the longest, the loudest, nor the smelliest fart, or the most in one day, month or year. In fact, surprisingly, it holds no statistics on the subject whatsoever. Never fear! From my own research into the subject of farting and through my attendance at the many farting conferences that are held each year throughout the world, I have come to the following reliable conclusions:

• Most of us pass somewhere between 200 and 2,000 ml of gas each and every day (that's an average of about 600 ml). An interesting thought for the next time that you breathe in a gulp of 'fresh' air.

• In one study I performed the results were that on average we pass wind 10–20 times a day, and in a study of men of about 20–40 years of age with healthily functioning bowels, the average number of gas eruptions was 16 times a day.

I have come across one study which makes a case for a man living in Oklahoma who farted as often as 145 times daily, including 83 farts in one four-hour period. I have yet to come across this human hurricane, but I would dearly love to meet him or anyone else that can make such an impressive claim.

There is a cheat's method to farting and that is to suck back in the air after letting go a fart and then to release it again. In this way one draws air back into the colon letting one fart and fart, and fart again.

Vital statistics:

It is possible to go a whole day without farting but in general my vital statistics are:

Average volume of passage of wind in healthy male:
- 600 ml

Average number of passages:
- Man: 15–17 farts in 24 hours
- Woman: 8–9 farts in 24 hours (OK they do it less but they do do it!)

Record statistics:
- 2,000 ml
- 145 farts in 24 hours
- 70 farts in 4 hours

Did you know?
- The average man releases enough flatus in a day to blow up a small balloon
- The war of farting between the sexes is equal on all matters of sound and smell

WHY ARE SOME FARTS NOISY AND SOME NOT?

Why are some farts honest and loud and others silent and deadly? One theory is based on diet:

Vegetarians

Vegetarians fart more often than meat-eaters because their diet is harder to digest. They also fart more quietly as all that roughage loosens the sphincter muscles. Just for the record, the farts do tend to be particularly offensive to the nostrils. For those who would like to have quiet farts, without turning veggie, let that air out very slowly and you might just get away with it.

Carnivores

Carnivores fart less than their veggie friends but, since they have tighter sphincters and go to the loo less often due to lack of roughage, they build up more pressure and hence are the greater reverberators. Squeezing the buttocks together may let out a fart bit by bit, but it can also result in a roaring blast. Be careful if you find yourself trying this in a lift or on a train at rush-hour.

WHY DO FARTS SMELL?

The disagreeable odour of flatus is caused by several sulphur compounds, particularly by mercaptans, (which are too complicated to explain here).

Everyone has a different mixture of gases causing different smells. Also, some farts will contain greater amounts of heavy gas so that they will hang around longer than others.

Did you know?
- Like all good perfumes, after two minutes farts become odourless to our noses
- If you fart into a bottle and put the cork back in, or into an airtight tin, you can preserve your ripest farts for some time – although I deem it very anti-social to do this in someone else's flask or lunchbox

WHAT IS THE LONGEST FART?

The time a fart hangs around depends on what foods one has eaten and how much gas was expelled. Farts can travel as far as fifteen metres and the smell can linger for two to five minutes, although I have also recorded twenty minutes.

HOT FARTS

The heat of the moment can be very embarrassing – yes, we all know the danger of hot farts! To understand why some farts are ringburners we need to go back to our internal chemistry lab. Basically, if you have a very full intestine, the particles inside rush round more quickly than usual and in the process produce heat which hots up our gas. Some foods such as curry and chilli also affect the heat in our intestines – hence the power of the good old curry fart.

The intestines are the home of tempests: in them is formed gas, as in the clouds

BRILLAT-SAVARIN

ARE BURPS THE SAME AS FARTS?

The exit of gas by mouth (eructation) or by anus (fart)

MEDICAL DEFINITION

Are burps the same as farts? Nope! Repeated belching indicates aerophagia. Some persons with this problem can readily produce a series of belches on command. This form of belching is due to unconscious, repeated aspiration of air into the oesophagus, often in response to stress, followed by rapid expulsion.

CAN YOU BURP AND FART AT THE SAME TIME?

This was a very good question sent in by 'Andrew H.'. He says that his friends have told him it is impossible, and, despite trying very hard, he has not been able to do it yet either. My researchers love a challenge and set to work immediately. Consumption of fizzy drinks and baked beans has been at its highest ever in our laboratory for many weeks now, but so far we have only been able to establish conclusively that it is possible to laugh and fart at the same time. Indeed, I am afraid that the laughter may have been hampering the results and we are therefore still trying to disprove the theory. If anyone has ever burped and farted at the same time, please e-mail me at **alec.bromcie@michaelomarabooks.com** explaining the circumstances of the occurrence, and any side-effects.

CAN YOU EVER SEE A FART?

In *The Complete Book of Farting*, I stated that farts are not visible unless you set light to them (which doesn't strictly speaking count). However, I have had a letter from Mrs Valerie Trumpington–Doody who writes:

> *When it is freezing outside and we breathe out hot air, we can see our breath quite clearly, so I was wondering whether if one farted outside in the freezing cold, could one see one's fart in the same way? I have yet to discover whether it is possible or not, as it's very difficult for one to turn round and see if one's fart is visible oneself. I suppose I could ask a friend, but I'm not sure anyone would take my request seriously . . . Please let me know your thoughts, and whether you plan to do any research into the subject.*

This is a very interesting theory, Mrs Trumpington–Doody, and one which my students are keen to research. Unfortunately, it has been particularly warm of late, here at the University of Valparaíso and we need funding to take a team of researchers to Alaska in order to find out if this theory has credence. If any reader can provide this funding, or indeed has carried out their own controlled experiments into this phenomenon, please contact me c/o my publisher.

HAS ANYONE EVER DIED FROM PASSING WIND?

Indirectly yes. There was a fatal case in Denmark where surgeons ignited a pocket of intestinal gases with an electrical surgical knife, causing major damage to the patient's internal organs which resulted in his death (more details can be found in *The History of Farting* by Dr Benjamin Bart and in my *The Complete Book of Farting*). I have also recently heard of a case where a patient in Paraguay suffered from such extreme constipation over a period of many days that he ate a large quantity of laxative and fart-inducing foods in the hope of 'forcing the issue'. Unfortunately, this did not work. His abdomen became distended, and the pressure on his lungs from the build-up of gases and stools would eventually have killed him, had it not been for the ingenuity of hospital staff who engineered a swift voidance and release of gases. (NB. Several bedpans later, the hospital doctor overseeing the 'cure' was so traumatized that he left the profession to become a shepherd.)

I have not been personally acquainted with anyone who has expired as a direct result of a particularly poisonous fart, or from the effort of forcing out an especially stubborn guff. However, if anyone has evidence to share, please contact me at the usual address.

CAN YOU TASTE A FART?

I have received a query from 'N.' as follows: 'If a fart is bad enough, would you be able to taste it? If so, would it taste of the last meal you ate?'

The senses of taste and smell are closely related – if you lose one sense, you often lose the other. Equally, if you can smell something, the taste is often influenced by the smell. (The only exception to this is herbal tea, which always smells far nicer than it actually tastes!) Therefore, in all the experiments my researchers and I have carried out, it has been very difficult to isolate a particular taste. We began our experiments by farting into specially designed containers which sealed in the fart. This enabled us to draw out the essence of the odour in empty syringes and inject the gas directly on to our tongues. Each of us ate a different food for a day before we began the tests and we held a 'blind tasting session'. We discovered that a fart created by eating nothing but eggs for 24 hours was identifiable by taste alone, but that baked beans, cabbage and fish were less easy to place. The eggy fart had (if I may borrow from wine-tasting terminology) overtones of the chicken yard, a sort of white earthy taste, and a hint of yolk. Cabbage was found to have a slatey flavour, baked beans were more reminiscent of tomatoes than beans, and fish created a subtle blend of charcoal and oysters.

MOTHER BROMCIE'S DINNER FARTY

Mother Bromcie
invites you to enjoy a seven-
course meal
to titillate your taste-buds and
invigorate your entire
digestive system.

Baked Eggs with Garlic

•

Chickpea, Tuscan Cabbage and
Pepperoni Soup

•

Chilli con Carne
Brown Rice
with an Accompaniment of Caraway
Coleslaw Deluxe

•

Fizzy Lemon Sherbet Sorbet

•

Spicy Mango Surprise

•

A Selection of Rare Stilton

•

Coffee & Cigars

•

Sugar-free After-dinner Mints

All recipes serve six, and should be
accompanied by a fine selection of
Belgian beers, so make sure your dining
room is well ventilated.

Baked Eggs with Garlic

Preheat oven to Gas Mark 6 (200°C, 400°F)

2 tablespoons extra virgin olive oil
3 fat cloves of garlic, finely chopped
6 sage leaves
6 large eggs
2 oz (50g) grated cheddar cheese
Salt and plenty of cayenne pepper

Prepare six ramekins by pouring the olive oil into each and swirling it around to coat fully. Share the chopped garlic between the six dishes and place a sage leaf in each. Break an egg into each ramekin and cover with a sprinkling of grated cheese. Place the ramekins on a baking tray and cook for 10 minutes. Remove from the oven, season and serve immediately.

Chickpea, Tuscan Cabbage and Pepperoni Soup

2 tablespoons olive oil
1 large onion
3 large garlic cloves
1 large red chilli
1 teaspoon Italian mixed herbs
4 oz (100g) pepperoni
1 red or yellow pepper
4 sticks celery
4 medium-sized potatoes
1 tablespoon flour
1³/₄ pints (1 litre) of chicken or vegetable stock
1 packet cavolo nero (Tuscan black cabbage)
14 oz (400g) can of chickpeas
salt & pepper
lemon juice

Thinly slice the onion and garlic, and finely chop the chilli.
Heat the oil in a heavy-based saucepan. Stir in the onion,
garlic and chilli together with the Italian herbs. Cook, stirring
every so often, over a medium-low heat until the onion has
softened and is beginning to brown.

Chop the pepperoni. De-seed and chop the pepper. Add the
pepperoni and pepper to the pan with 1 teaspoon of salt and
stir. While this mixture is cooking, slice the celery thinly and
dice the potatoes into small cubes. Add the celery and
potatoes to the pan, stir thoroughly and cover. Leave the
mixture to sweat over a very low heat for 5 minutes, stirring
occasionally.

Shake the flour into the vegetable mixture and stir until incorporated. Add the stock. Bring to the boil and leave to simmer uncovered for about 10 minutes until all the vegetables are tender. Taste the soup and season with salt and lemon juice. Tip the chickpeas into a sieve and rinse. Shred the cabbage, discarding the tough stalks. Add the chickpeas to the pan.

Return to the boil and add the cabbage. Cook for 3 minutes. Serve with plenty of black pepper.

Chilli con Carne

1 teaspoon vegetable oil
1^1/$_2$ lbs (600g) minced beef
1 large onion, peeled and chopped
^{1}/$_2$ green pepper, seeded and chopped
14 oz (400g) can tomatoes, chopped
salt and pepper
1 tablespoon chilli powder
1 teaspoon brown sugar
2 tablespoons tomato purée
14 oz (400g) can of red kidney beans

Fry the minced beef in oil until lightly browned, add the onion and pepper and fry for 5 minutes until soft. Blend together the chilli powder, brown sugar and tomato purée. Stir in the tomatoes, chilli paste and seasoning, add the kidney beans, and simmer for 30 minutes, stirring occasionally.

To cook the brown rice, allow 2-3 oz (50-75g) per person, place in a casserole dish with 1^1/$_2$ times water (e.g. 3 fl oz (75ml) water per 2 oz (50g) rice) and salt, and cook at Gas Mark 5 (190°C, 375°F) for 45 minutes or until all the water has been absorbed and the rice is tender.

Caraway Coleslaw Deluxe

1 white cabbage
4 carrots
1 medium-sized onion
4 tablespoons mayonnaise
4 tablespoons salad cream
1 teaspoon caraway seeds
lemon juice
salt and pepper

Finely slice all the vegetables and mix in a serving bowl.
Blend the mayonnaise, salad cream and caraway seeds, and add
lemon juice and seasoning to taste. Mix into the vegetables
and refrigerate until required.

Fizzy Lemon Sherbet Sorbet

4 oz (100g) granulated sugar
4 fl oz (100ml) water
Zest, juice and pulp of 2 lemons
3 fl oz (75ml) orange juice
packet of sherbet

Dissolve the sugar in the water in a saucepan. Bring to the
boil then simmer for 10 minutes to make a syrup. Allow to
cool fully and mix in the zest, juice and pulp of the lemons
and the orange juice. Put the mixture in a suitable container,
cover and freeze until slushy, for about one hour. Transfer the
mixture to a food processor with a metal blade and process
until smooth, or stir vigorously with a metal spoon. Put back
into the container, cover and freeze for a further hour. At this
point, stir briefly, fold in the sherbet and freeze for a further
hour. Serve garnished with curls of lemon peel.

Spicy Mango Surprise

3 mangoes
5 teaspoons icing sugar
1 teaspoon mild chilli powder

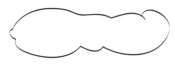

Slice the mangoes in half, avoiding the flattish stone inside. Make deep criss-cross slashes through the flesh of the mango but not all the way through the skin, creating a grid of squares about $1/2$ inch (1cm). When each half has been cut, you should be able to turn each one inside out, like a hedgehog. Combine the chilli powder and icing sugar, and sprinkle on to each mango half. Grill for 5-10 minutes under a medium heat until the icing sugar starts to caramelize. Serve with double cream.

Selection of Rare Stilton, Coffee, Cigars and Mints

Ensure that the Stilton is extremely mature, and make sure that it has been kept at room temperature for at least 48 hours prior to serving. Serve the coffee as strong as possible, as this loosens the bowels and sets the fart process in motion. Smoking cigars is a great way to swallow the amounts of air necessary to create pleasing farts. Sugar-free mints are best, as they have a laxative effect when eaten in large quantities. Keep passing them around!

Mother Bromcie always likes to make her guests feel at home by creating a very special atmosphere in which to dine. Her dog, Guffy The Brownfires Layer (pedigree name), always sits under the table. As Guffy is very old and pretty smelly, Mother Bromcie's more inhibited guests can relax in the knowledge that they can blame the dog if they let off a smelly one. A dry-ice machine in the corner of the room and a whoopee cushion on each chair soon have the guests feeling relaxed, and, if it is a special occasion, Mother Bromcie puts out stink-bomb crackers for her guests to take home. Suggested mood music includes:

'Be Proud Be Loud (Be Heard)' – Toyah

'Fanfare for the Common Man' – Emerson, Lake & Palmer

'Distant Drums' – Jim Reeves

'Both Ends Burning' – Roxy Music

'Can't Keep It In' – Cat Stevens

'The Air That I Breathe' – The Hollies

'Don't Try to Stop It' - Roman Holiday

'Classical Gas' – Mason Williams

'Blowin' In The Wind' – Peter, Paul & Mary

or anything by the Pat Methaney Group

Here is a public service announcement . . .

The advice below is from instructions to passengers issued by a British airline in 1926, when commercial flying was in its infancy, and aircraft were not pressurized.

High-fliers should empty their bladder before leaving and should not eat such food as peas, beans and brown bread, which are apt to cause formation of gas in the intestines.

FARTING ETIQUETTE

BENDING THE RULES

Since I wrote *The Complete Book of Farting*, many women (including a disproportionate number of policewomen) have written in to give their viewpoint on farting etiquette. As a result, I have had to bend some of my own rules on this matter.

It has been asserted by most female readers that women s*hould* fart on a first date (I advised against this previously), as it is a very good way of finding out about your partner. If he is a gentleman, he will pretend not to have noticed. If, however, he immediately grasps his throat and nose and pretends to collapse choking to the floor, you would be advised to be 'washing your hair' in the unlikely event that he calls for a second date. However, if your date applauds and calls for more beer, you have found a real soul mate. After all, you've got to get these things aired at some point in the relationship.

40

Personally, I still maintain that women should be careful whilst on a first date. Please take extra care if you are on a diet. It is all very well munching on high fibre crispbreads and salads for several weeks in order to fit into that strappy little dress for your hot date, but once the effects of the diet are gusting around the car when he gratefully drops you home, all your hard work will have been wasted.

Equally, if you do attempt to squeeze into that pair of tight leather trousers, beware of their constricting nature. All that pressure on your stomach will have to be released sometime. Also, remember that no man wants to see your tights ballooning so early in the relationship…

Then again, if your man takes you for a night out on the lager, followed by a curry of which he fully expects you to partake, he does not deserve your abstinence fartwise. Remember, two farts eat as one, or if you can't beat 'em, join 'em!

If you find yourself in a particularly comfortable relationship, in which you may be able to beat him at a farting contest any day of the week, remember that in public you can still blame him for your 'social errors'. Most men will not want the world to know that their girlfriends are diabolically disgusting farters. Moreover, they will not want to admit that you are better at farting than them, especially in front of their mates, (although one or two women have written in to tell me that their men positively laud their flatulent abilities).

I am afraid I have to bring up the subject of fanny farts. Again. I reiterate, if the affair has already reached the point of freefall farting, then there should be no problem. However, if it has not, this practice may come as a great shock to some men. I received a letter from a rather distressed young woman who fanny-farted during her first sexual encounter with her new boyfriend. He was so shocked that he jumped out of bed and ran out of the door, and she hasn't seen him since. This is not the best way to deal with the problem, chaps. Ladies, fart warily and do try not to surprise him too soon. Men, should an involuntary rasp occur during lovemaking, be a man and neither recoil in horror – NOR laugh. Be sensitive to how your partner may be feeling and either ignore the parp or reassure your loved one. This way you can laugh long and loud about it with your mates for years to come.

Farting in the gym or at an aerobics class often causes women consternation. However, before you go ahead, make sure you consider the ambient temperature of the room, your proximity to other exercisers and the direction of any fan or air-conditioning that may be in the room. All these will have a bearing on whether it will be smelt or not. As for noise, there are certain stretched positions that will angle your cheeks and enable you to fart soundlessly, but you will need to experiment with these in the privacy of your own home to work out what is best for you.

Farting in the swimming pool is to be avoided in case you find you are in one of those public baths with a colourant to show if someone pees. Do you want to take the risk of letting something else out which will then prove your guilt? However, if you are confident of releasing only wind, make sure you are doing something splashy with your legs to disguise the bubbles.

Remember, farting naked on an inflatable plastic chair is a practice which should only be carried out in the privacy of your own home.

And finally, a note on pamphing, which is the practice of sniffing someone else's recently vacated seat. It is particularly useful for getting tables in crowded pubs – simply wait until one of the people seated at the table of your choice gets up, preferably to go to the toilet, then go up and explore their still-warm chair with your nose, shouting out to your friends, 'Here's one!' Usually the occupants of the table will be so disgusted that they will get up and leave, whereupon you and your friends can relax in comfort at their table for the rest of the evening.

THE FARTING ZODIAC

My astrologist sister, Alicia Bromcie, helps you find your farting soul mate

Aries (21st March to 20th April)

- Competitive
- Adventurous and energetic
- Pioneering and courageous
- Enthusiastic and confident
- Foolhardy and daredevil

Arien subjects are courageous leaders and as such they are the first in a room to let rip. As followers they can be troublesome and will sulk if someone beats them off the mark. In their personal relationships, Ariens are frank and direct and make good friends. If you are too shy to fart first, get together with an Aries who will lead the way for you.

Taurus (21st April to 21st May)

- Practical
- Artistic
- Idealistic
- Patient and reliable
- Persistent and determined
- Jealous and possessive
- Resentful and inflexible
- Self-indulgent and greedy

The Bull, and boy, do these people want you to know they are the dog's bollocks when it comes to farting. Even his or her farts have got to be bigger and smellier than anyone else's. Female Taureans even boast to their friends that their fanny farts are the loudest in the kingdom. They also take pride in their farts lingering longer. If you enjoy the smell of farts, hang around a Taurus. But remember, they are jealous and self-indulgent, so do not try to compete. These people usually work in marketing or some other aggressive job. They should live miles from anyone and not on the fifth floor of a block of flats, as when they start to blow off, buildings shake and young children hide under their blankets. If this does not put you off then nothing will.

Gemini (22nd May to 21st June)

- Well-informed
- Adaptable and versatile
- Communicative and witty
- Intellectual and eloquent
- Superficial and inconsistent
- Cunning and inquisitive

Gemini, the sign of the Twins, is two-faced, elusive, complex and contradictory. On the one hand it produces the virtue of versatility, and on the other the vices of two-facedness and flightiness. Therefore, they usually fart in crowds so they can pin the blame on someone else and run away. Since Geminis are great communicators they can fart a whole range of sounds with different intensities. Their pitch and tone is music to our ears.

Cancer (22nd June to 23rd July)

- House-proud
- Clan-conscious (basically maternal)
- Intuitive and imaginative
- Shrewd and cautious
- Protective and sympathetic
- Changeable and moody
- Over-emotional and touchy

The Cancerian character is the least clear-cut of all those associated with the signs of the zodiac. Among farters they are the most charming exponents of this art. They are very at ease with their bodily functions but can be moody sometimes. This leads to them getting upset when members of their family let loose with a blaster. A Cancerian will also come to your defence if somebody else takes the fun out of your farts. They are most relaxed in the company of Taureans and should seek out this star sign if looking for a soul mate.

Leo (24th July to 23rd August)

- Confident
- Dignified
- Intimidates others easily
- Generous and warm-hearted
- Creative and enthusiastic
- Broad-minded and expansive
- Pompous and patronizing
- Bossy and interfering
- Dogmatic

The Leo type is the most dominant, spontaneously creative and extrovert of all the zodiacal characters. They are the monarchs among humans as the lion is king of beasts. They love to be the centre of attention, which makes for a fun time if they are surrounded by Taureans. They love it when one of their farts gets people talking and will patronize anyone whose fart does not measure up. Leos do have a generous side and enjoy being asked to perform. If you ask politely to smell it they will love you for ever.

Virgo (24th August to 23rd September)

- Body-conscious
- Modest and shy
- Intelligent and analytical
- Fussy and a worrier
- Over-critical and harsh
- Perfectionist and conservative

Virgo is the only zodiacal sign represented by a female. On the surface Virgoans are cold and some may say anally retentive. Because of this they are the last in a room to drop a fart. If you can convince a Virgo to drop one you are in for a treat. Because they are shy and are worried by what their bodies do, they tend to hold them in far longer than they should. Consequently the smell of their farts will wake the dead.

Libra (24th September to 23rd October)

- Diplomatic
- Attractive
- Fair
- Urbane
- Romantic and charming
- Easy-going and sociable
- Idealistic and peaceable

Libra is the only inanimate sign of the zodiac. Librans have elegance, charm and good taste, are kind, very gentle, and lovers of beauty. Because of this they tend not to get involved in rowdy farting contests but do their farting in private. They absolutely die of shame if accused of dropping one and feel that the whole farting process is practised by other people. However, in a long-term relationship their guard goes down and they unload the sweetest farts imaginable. They are most at home with Virgoans.

Scorpio (24th October to 22nd November)

- Powerful
- Passionate
- Intense
- Jealous and resentful
- Compulsive and obsessive
- Secretive and obstinate

Scorpios are the most intense, powerful characters in the zodiac. Even when they appear self-controlled and calm there is a seething well of emotional energy underneath the placid exterior. They are like volcanoes and their farts reflect this. Their farts have a sting in the tail and you never know when they will let one out. Never hold a contest between Leos and Scorpios. They will fart to the death.

Sagittarius (23rd November to 21st December)

- Adventurous
- Funny
- Knowledgeable
- Eternally optimistic
- Freedom-loving
- Jovial and good-humoured
- Intellectual and philosophical

Sagittarians have a positive outlook on life, are full of enterprise, energy, versatility and eagerness. They enjoy travelling and exploration. They are always looking for new thrills and will be the first in a room to light their fart and tell you exactly what they ate to cause such a firestorm. They can smell a fart and tell you what you have eaten and will know everything about the composition of the fart. If you want to find someone who will show an interest in your farts then this star sign will make your perfect partner. Their philosophical side is immense and their favourite saying is 'I fart, therefore I am'.

Capricorn (22nd December to 20th January)

- Patient
- Practical
- Ambitious and disciplined
- Humorous and reserved
- Fatalistic
- Miserly and grudging

The Capricorn is one of the most down-to-earth and serious of the zodiacal types. These independent characters have many qualities, although admittedly some of these are dull. A Capricorn's fart slips out of his or her arse more smoothly and more slippily than an eel on a hook. Because they are disciplined they will not fart at will, but store them up and only release one so as to achieve the maximum effect. This star sign is prone to anal leakage and you should be aware of this if you intend to spend much time in bed with one. They are full of surprises, however, and very funny.

Aquarius (21st January to 19th February)

- Unusual
- Well-intentioned
- Stubborn
- Friendly
- Honest
- Original and inventive
- Intractable and contrary
- Perverse and unpredictable

The Water Bearer, like Capricorn, suffers from wet farts that will test the absorbent nature of their underwear to the hilt. If male they never wear light trousers, and female Aquarians never go far from home without finding out that there are toilet facilities en route beforehand. They have a breadth of vision that is quite awe-inspiring. If you are looking for farts that are totally unique then this is the sign to watch out for.

Pisces (20th February to 20th March)

- Sensitive
- Imaginative
- Hopelessly sentimental
- Potential for mind-altering drug addictions
- Exaggerates everything

Pisces is one of the less flashy signs and their farts are more ordinary than those of, for example, Leo, Scorpio and Aquarius. However, they have an addictive nature and indeed some people swear that they get a high from sniffing one of their explosions. The magic-mushroom fart is a favourite and if the donor has eaten baked beans as well, the results are like having an LSD trip. Strange colours and strange objects float by those who are downwind of these farts. As long as you go with the flow then no long-term damage is sustained. Be warned that Piscean farters are genuinely fishy farters, and are prone to embellish the truth and just love sitting around telling tales of their farting exploits.

WINDWARD HO!

We all know the penalties for being drunk in charge of a vehicle, but being flatulent in charge of a ship?

The skipper of a research ship which ran aground off the Florida coast voluntarily surrendered his licence to the coastguard and asked to be relieved of his duties. Investigators were initially told that he had sneezed and had a blackout, which caused him temporarily to lose control of his vessel. Unfortunately the truth was somewhat different. Apparently, the captain had dropped a fart of such mammoth proportions in the close quarters of the wheelhouse that he and both his colleagues had had to go out on to the bridge wing in order to regain their breath… which was when the accident happened . . .

(Thanks to M Fisher and Andrew Linington of NUMAST journal for this story)

FARTERS ANONYMOUS: MORE TRUE FARTING CONFESSIONS

Many people have written to me since I published *The Complete Book of Farting*; some are embarrassed about their farting and want to cover it up, some of them want to stand up and be counted as farters, but they all have stories to tell.

In their honour, I have printed a selection of their confessions here.

Hi, my name is Dave, and I'm a farter. In the mornings, my family and I all get in the car to drop off the children with the childminder, and then my wife gives me a lift to the station before she drives off to her own work. Now, in the morning my guts are often in turmoil and it is not unknown for me to let rip on the way to the station. When this happens, I open the window and wave the offending whiff out of the car, and apart from a comment from my wife about how gross I am, there normally isn't a problem – until recently when we endured a rather cold spell of weather.

We went through the usual routine, and then on the way to the station, I let out one of my 'guess who had a curry last night?' specials, which was even more sulphurous than usual and which seemed to take the oxygen out of the air. Seeing as my wife was complaining so much and threatening to throw up, I thought I ought to open the window and usher it out. I pressed the button to open the electric windows only to find that the cold weather had frozen them up, and we couldn't open any of the windows or even the sun-roof. We were trapped with my eggy odours for about another ten minutes before the car warmed up enough to open a window and let in some much-needed fresh air, by which time my wife had gone a rather strange shade of green. Anyway, from now on I am banned from farting in the car unless I test the windows first.

Dave P

Hello, I'm Rick and I'm a farter. I have a friend who, for some medical reason best known to Mother Nature, cannot burp. This is a genetic disorder passed down on his father's side, and he has a brother with the same problem. Therefore, with only one escape route for tummy bubbles, you can begin to imagine the multitude of farts I have witnessed being emitted by our combustible companion. One day, myself and another friend were trying to outfart one another, as teenagers generally do. I had amassed a humble thirteen emissions within 35 minutes, and my counterpart was on about eleven, and gaining. Enter my biologically-gifted friend, and within 22 minutes (accurately timed due to amazement), he had violated our nostrils with 32 cheek-splitters! Meanwhile our bottoms were silenced in the presence of such an omnipotent, awe-inspiring arse!

Rick M

Hi, I'm Michael, and I'm a farter. I want to tell you about my religious experience. Because I was older and the parish school did not have enough room to have all of us attend Sunday School in the morning, I was one of the kids who took my religion classes in the evening. This naturally meant that I ate dinner before I went to school, and this one particular evening my mom gave me a lot of sausage and sauerkraut.

I went to the parish school and sat down in the next-to-the-back row of the classroom away from everybody else because I didn't know many of the other kids. Behind me sat one other student. An hour into the session the class was discussing God intensely when I felt a tremendous rumbling deep in my butt. I knew that this was going to be a bad one if I let it go, and for five minutes I almost broke a sweat trying to push the thing back up my bum, because the class was absolutely quiet and hanging on every word of the instructor. After a while I felt the pressure relieve itself, and the fart seemingly disappeared back up into my gut. I breathed a sigh of relief and at last I relaxed my arse cheeks.

The moment I relaxed myself, the entire built-up fart came barrelling out of my bum at unholy speed and blasted its full pent-up force on to the wooden chair beneath me. The way it blasted on to the chair and echoed off the concrete walls created a roar so loud and ear-shattering that you would have thought God himself was walking into the back of the classroom.

The entire class stopped its discussion and all heads turned around to look at me. Every face in Sunday School was staring right at me and the student sitting behind me, because we were the only ones who could have done it. For a split second I didn't know what to do because I was in total shock at what had happened. The kids were saying to themselves, 'Good God!', 'Holy cow!' and anything else that could describe their disbelief.

And then Divine Inspiration struck: I immediately turned around and stared at the boy sitting behind me along with all the other students. He was wide-eyed, and looking back at the entire class he loudly announced, 'Really, I did NOT do that!' I just shook my head at 'his' fart and turned around, looking at the other students and saying, 'Oh no . . .!', and none of the other pupils ever suspected me. I have been a devout Christian ever since.

Michael S

Hi, my name is Gary, and I'm a musical farter. Every night in bed, I get a gurgling in my stomach, and as I breathe out, an enormous vibration hits my rectum and goes from a pleasant woodwind to an erratic percussion sound.

Gary K

Hi, I'm Jenny, and I'm not a farter. A friend of mine, who is in the Territorial Army, called me after his last drill. One of the women in his group has an 11-year-old daughter, and when Mum was dropped off at drill that Friday, the daughter threw a wobbly. When she was reprimanded, the daughter replied 'Mum, women aren't allowed to fart, burp or snore. If we don't have hissy fits, we'll explode!'

Jenny C

Hi, My name is Felicity, and I am definitely a farter. About ten years ago, I was working for a pizza-delivery company. It was nearly closing time, and everything was really quiet. There were other employees sitting down waiting to close up, and I was standing up in front of the huge windows at the front of the shop cleaning them. All of a sudden, the cook decided to come up behind me and poke me in the ribs as I was cleaning the windows. I let out the biggest fart; it scared me so much. Needless to say, everyone burst into laughter. It was never the same there again.

Felicity P

Hi, I'm Darren and I'm a farter. About a year ago I was at the video shop near my home. Shortly after entering the shop I felt the tell-tale rumbling of a real winner in the brewery. I instinctively knew it would be a bad one because I had eaten corned beef and cabbage for lunch; I love the stuff but it doesn't love me. After a few minutes I had worked my way to the letter 'C' in new releases and my fart had moved to the starting gate and was ready to run. I looked around and there was nobody near so I let it out silently. I knew it was a bad one because of the arse-burn upon release. I waited a moment for it to get out of my pants, patted my wallet to get rid of any residue and quickly moved to the 'K' section of the new releases looking at videos with one eye and keeping the other eye on the 'C' section.

After a few moments a female employee walked directly to the section to replace a video. As she was reaching towards the shelf, my landmine exploded. She froze in place, then dropped the video and started gagging and sprinting towards the staff toilet. I tried to keep a straight face and continue my video search, but I wasn't successful, and I ended up laughing so hard that tears were coming out of my eyes. Eventually I got myself under control, found a video and went to the checkout counter where I almost made a good escape. While a male employee was checking my card, the accosted female employee returned to the checkout counter still looking a little green around the gills. At that point I started laughing uncontrollably all over again so the female employee guessed it was me on the spot. I tried to apologize but was laughing too hard to do so. The male employee must have been told what happened and asked me, 'Was that you?' I could only nod. He replied, 'Well done! She's a complete bitch!'
Darren A

Hello, I'm Tom, and my friend is a farter. My friend and I were in a maths lesson when the teacher said she could smell a digusting smell which was interfering with her lesson. It did not go away as my friend kept farting and eventually the teacher opened the windows and said they were to stay open until the smell had gone. We all froze, until my friend gave in and the teacher told him if it happened again he would be put in solitary confinement and his parents would be telephoned.

Tom W

Hi, I'm Ally, and my friend is a farter. She treats farting as a sport, and her favourite event is the Sooper Whooper Pooper, where she stands on a chair, lifts up her skirt and farts out the tune to *EastEnders*. Unfortunately, as in any sport, there are dangers, and after a fart-lighting event went wrong last year, she was admitted to hospital with severe burns to her privates and frazzled hair to match.

Ally C

Hi, my name's Mike, and I'm definitely a farter. When I was a boy in the Scouts, I had to attend church for the much-dreaded Church Parade. Being a lad who quite enjoyed his greens, I used to have trouble controlling my emissions, and would try and delay the inevitable for as long as possible. Unfortunately, this made things worse, as I always ended up 'letting go' as we were listening to the vicar say prayers, which of course is when the church is at its quietest. Pews are not the best type of seating to smother the sound of ejections, and mine used to reverberate round the church, much to the amusement of all the Cubs and Scouts present, who used to burst into fits of giggles, while I went redder than a fire engine . . .

Mike F

Hi, my name's Scott, and I'm a farter. As a naval officer, I spend a lot of time on board ship, and I love to entertain the crew by sharing my very individual farts with them. This is easy to achieve as I simply go into the air-conditioning room and fart straight into the fan intake. This enables me to share with my fellow sailors the joys of the navy diet.

Scott M

Hello, I'm Zak, and I'm a lazy farter. One day, I was out with my mates in the pub when I farted. It wasn't too bad a fart, but unfortunately, I followed through. The smell was lingering really badly but I couldn't be bothered to go home and change. I went into the gents and pulled down my pants, and sure enough, there was a nasty brown stain. I got out my lighter and burned through the crotch of my pants at both ends to remove the dirty part, but since I didn't think it would flush, I hid the smelly bit behind the cistern. No one dared remove it for weeks and it might even still be there! I just carried on drinking with my mates and I didn't care when they took the piss out of me for being so idle and disgusting!

Zak H

Hi, I'm Ricky, and I'm definitely a farter. I used to fart all the time without thinking much of it, but when I was at university, my girlfriend and all my housemates started to complain so much that my farts were really disgusting, I became convinced that I had a medical problem. I went to the doctor who said that there were certain complaints which caused severe flatulence and he proceeded to carry out all the tests. After weeks of worrying and waiting (and farting), I went back to the doctor for the test results and he said that he had good news and bad news. Naturally I asked for the good news first and was told that there was nothing wrong with me. The bad news was, of course, that I'm just a smelly farter! I was rather embarrassed to say the least.

Ricky C

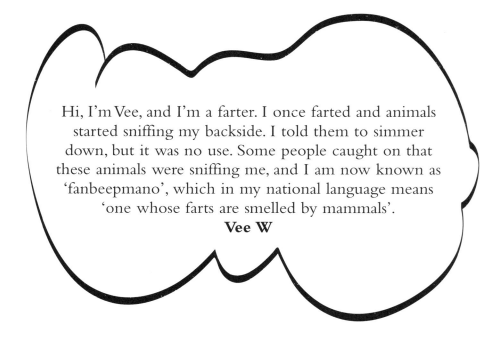

Hi, I'm Vee, and I'm a farter. I once farted and animals started sniffing my backside. I told them to simmer down, but it was no use. Some people caught on that these animals were sniffing me, and I am now known as 'fanbeepmano', which in my national language means 'one whose farts are smelled by mammals'.

Vee W

Feel free to send your true farting stories to me at my publishers or at: **alec.bromcie@michaelomarabooks.com.** Your story may appear in a future edition. We will let you know if we are going to use it.

TAKING THE MIKEY

The acclaimed BBC foreign correspondent, John Simpson, reveals the danger of farting whilst wearing a microphone. Here he gives us the bottom line on Colonel Gaddhafi of Libya.

That evening, back in the hotel, I rang the office while Bob went carefully through the interview making sure everything was all right. He came into my room with the camera and a viewing monitor. 'There are some noises on it,' he said.

'What kind of noises?'

I was worried. Once before, in Iraq, I had filmed an interview in an army base and the pictures were ruined by electronic interference.

'Kind of personal noises.'

I am very fond indeed of Bob, and know him quite well by now. In particular, I know how modest he is about bodily functions.

'What do you mean? Burping, farting, that kind of thing?'

'Farting,' he said, without looking at me.

71

'*Absolute crap. I was sitting two feet away from him, and I didn't hear anything.*'

'*Listen on the headphones. I picked it up on his personal mike.*'

It was there all right, on one long section of the interview: ten absolutely unmistakable minutes of the Leader breaking wind long and loudly as he spoke. The small microphone pinned to his Hawaiian shirt had caught the sound perfectly. Not only that, but you could see him lifting himself up out of his seat in familiar, tell-tale fashion, and sinking back each time with a discreet smile. If you are the Leader, you can wear what you want, write what you want, and fart when you want. No one is going to tell you otherwise.

From *A Mad World My Masters*, John Simpson, 2000; Macmillan, London

FARTING VERSE –
or worse . . .

There was an old major from Fife
Who doggedly looked for a wife.
Though so hard he tried
He was always denied
On account of his flatulent life.

A talented fellow from Crete
Could fart to a rhythmical beat.
His abilities wowed;
Of this he was proud.
His was such a remarkable feat.

There once was a tragic self-starter
Whose farting produced lots of laughter.
On a diet of leeks
He parped daily for weeks,
Then dropped dead, the poor gaseous martyr.

There was a young woman from Worcester,
Whose breezes would never pass muster.
She tried every week
To emit more than a squeak
But her efforts would always disgust her.

A gardener hailing from Leeds
Would fart when he stooped to pick weeds.
He'd fluff when he hoed,
Blow off when he mowed
And let rip when he bent to plant seeds.

There was an old lady from Sale
Who could fart like a flatulent whale.
Like typhoons they'd blow,
When lit how they'd glow.
Her secret? A diet of ale.

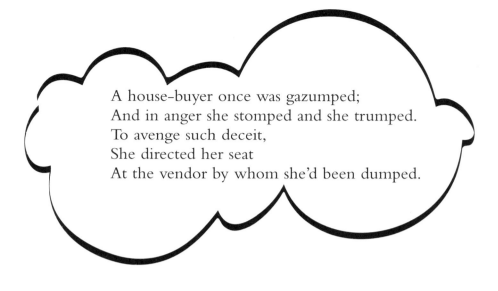

A house-buyer once was gazumped;
And in anger she stomped and she trumped.
To avenge such deceit,
She directed her seat
At the vendor by whom she'd been dumped.

There once was a golfer from Crieff
Whose flatulence caused him much grief.
His drives went sky-high,
His putting awry,
While his cheeks produced queef after queef.

There was a young doctor from Stoke
Whose farts caused his patients to choke.
When his rear end did mutter,
They'd cough and they'd splutter
Then they'd flee from the stench, the poor folk.

There once was a caddie called Carter
Whose wife was a bit of a tartar.
She'd feed him on beans
And three-week-old greens,
Which made him World Champion Farter.

Limericks courtesy of Helen Blowers, with a special contribution from Ripper Ron

AN ODE TAE A FERT

Oh what a sleekit horrible beastie
Lurks in yer belly efter the feastie
Just as ye sit doon among yer kin
There sterts to stir an enormous wind

The neeps and tatties and mushy peas
stert workin like a gentle breeze
but soon the puddin wi the sauncie face
will have ye blawin all ower the place

Nae matter whit the hell ye dae
a'bodys gonnae have tae pay
even if ye try to stifle
It's like a bullet oot a rifle

Hawd yer bum tight tae the chair
tae try and stop the leakin air
shify yersel fae cheek tae cheek
Prae tae God it doesnae reek

But aw yer efforts go assunder
oot it comes like a clap a thunder
Ricochets aroon the room
michty me a sonic boom

God almighty it fairly reeks
Hope I huvnae shit ma breeks
tae the bog I better scurry
aw whit the hell, it's no ma worry

A'body roon aboot me chokin
wan or two are nearly bokin
I'll feel better for a while
Cannae help but raise a smile

Wis him! I shout with accusin glower
alas too late, he's just keeled ower
Ye dirty bugger they shout and stare
A dinnae feel welcome any mair

Where e're ye go let yer wind gan' free
sounds like just the job fur me
whit a fuss at Rabbie's perty
ower the sake o' won wee ferty

This poem was sent to me anonymously and I was so chuffed
I just had to share it with my farting friends. However, I don't
want to cause a stink, so if you wrote it and would like
recognition for this fine contribution to farting literature,
please contact me c/o my publisher.

THE GREAT FARTING CONTEST

I will tell you a tale that is certain to please,
Of a great farting contest at Shitham on Pease,
When all the great arses paraded the fields,
To take part in a contest for various shields.

Some cocked up their arses to fart up the scale,
To strive for a cup and a barrel of ale.
And those whose arses were biggest and strongest,
Took part in the contest for loudest and longest.

This pleasant event had drawn a great crowd,
And the betting was even on Mrs McLoud.
It was said in the papers, the sporting edition,
That this lady's arse was in perfect condition.

Now old Mrs Potluck was backed for a place,
For she had often been placed in the deepest disgrace,
Having farted in church and drowned the great organ,
And gassed the old verger, Marmaduke Morgan.

With a clump of red hairs and a wart on each side,
She cocked it up well with the greatest of pride.
She fancied her chance of winning with ease,
Having trained on a diet of cabbage and peas.

The vicar arrived and ascended the stand,
And proceeded to tell this remarkable band,
That the contest was on as was shown on the bills,
And the use was taboo of injections and pills.

The contestants lined up at the signal to start,
And winning the toss Mrs Jones took first fart.
The crowd were astonished in silence and wonder,
And the BBC issued a warning of thunder.

Next Mrs Black who advanced to the front,
And started by doing a wonderful stunt.
With wide parted cheeks and tightly clenched hands,
She blew off the roof of the sixpenny stands.

Old Mrs Potluck thought nothing of this,
She'd had some weak tea and was all wind and piss.
With hands on her hips and legs stretched out wide,
she unluckily shit and was disqualified.

Next Mrs Bugle who farted alone,
And the crowd were amazed at the sweetness of her
tone.
The judges agreed without bias of pause,
First prize Mrs Bugle, now pull up your drawers.

She advanced to the rostrum with maidenly gait,
To receive from the vicar a set of gold plate.
Then she farted to the crowd who had started to sing,
And farted to the first verse of 'God Save The King'.

This poem was sent to me by Stewart Bratt, who has had it in
his possession for over 40 years, but he doesn't know its origin.
If anyone can shed any light on this, please contact me.

NO LAUGHING MATTER

More of the best farting jokes around!

Why do men fart more than women?
Because women can't shut up long enough to build up the required pressure.

There are two men sitting in a hunting club. One says to the other, 'I think it's spelled W-H-H-O-O-O-M-B.'

The other man replies, 'No, wouldn't it be more like W-H-H-H-O-O-M-M-B-B?'

The waitress is walking by and says, 'You guys are both idiots! It's spelled W-O-M-B, you jerks!' and she storms off.

The first man turns to his friend and says, 'Well, wouldn't you know it? She's heard an elephant fart too!'

A man goes to visit his doctor.

'Doctor, I've got a rather embarrassing problem, my farts just don't sound right.'

'Well, how do they sound?' enquires the doctor.

'They've started making a "HONDA" noise.'
The doctor looks puzzled. 'Hmm, is there anything else I should know?'

'Well, I also have a terrible boil on my bum,' replies the man.
The doctor looks pleased. 'That's it then. We'll lance that boil and you'll see a difference immediately.'

'How on earth could that possibly work?' asks the man.

'It's a well-known fact,' the Doctor tells him. 'Abscess makes the fart go Honda.'

A man goes to the doctor.

'Well [fart] Doctor, I [fart] just can't stop [fart] farting, [fart] it's driving me [fart] mad [fart]!'

The doctor nods and says,

'Ok, wait here a minute,' and he walks over to the corner of the room and picks up a long stick with a hook on the end of it. The man looks worried.

'[fart] Oh, my [fart] God, doctor, is [fart] that going [fart] to [fart] hurt much?'

The doctor shakes his head.

'No,' he says. 'I'm going to open the window, it stinks in here!'

(Thanks to Ducky for sending me this joke – she says she wishes she had this problem, although she's not sure how long her mates would stand by her. Well, according to the research in *The Complete Book of Farting*, the maximum distance a fart can travel is 15 metres, so long as they stand across the street, you can still be friends!)

A young man is coming home from a nightclub with a lady for the first time. He's never had sex before and knows nothing about 'these things'. The lady says to him, 'Just relax, I'm gonna do what is called a 69er'. This sounds okay so he tries it out. A few seconds into it the lady rips off the hugest fart, but before she can apologize, the young man gets up and walks out, saying 'Stuff this, I can't handle another 68 of those!'

Two English couples are standing in the pub. One of the men farts very loudly and the other one says, 'Sir, you just passed wind before my wife!' The first man says, 'Sorry, old bean, I didn't realize it was her turn!'

An old Italian woman is going up in the elevator in a very lavish New York office building.

A young and beautiful woman gets into the elevator and, smelling of expensive perfume, turns to the old Italian woman and says arrogantly, 'Giorgio Beverly Hills, $100 an ounce!'

Another young and beautiful woman gets into the lift and also very arrogantly turns to the old Italian woman and says, 'Chanel No. 5, $150 an ounce!'

About three floors later, the old Italian woman has reached her destination and is about to get out of the elevator. Before she leaves, she looks both beautiful women in the eye, bends over, and farts, saying, 'Broccoli, 49 cents a pound.'

THE FUTURE OF FARTING

During the last year, my fellow fartologists and I have been carrying out research into all the latest scientific advances in this wonderful pastime, and also into its serious uses. We have devised a standard system of measurement for farts, The Bleaufart Scale, and hope that this will be adopted as an industry standard. We have been using the scale to catalogue different parts of the world and our results follow shortly.

First of all, I want to introduce our most important breakthrough: can farting solve one of the world's greatest problems?

FARTS: THE FUEL OF THE FUTURE?

In my previous bestseller I described how the farts of cows and sheep were destroying the ozone layer over the South Pole and endangering our very existence on this planet. Fortunately, when scientists read my book, they leapt into action and produced a scheme which will reverse this trend. In fact, farting will save the world!

This is how the plan works: cows and sheep worldwide will have large balloons connected to their bums to collect the methane gas which is damaging the ozone layer. The gas will be collected daily, piped into much larger balloons and brought to transport centres where it will be transferred to zeppelins for shipment around the world. The beauty of the scheme is that the lighter–than–air methane will both send the zeppelins into the skies and fuel the gas-powered engines. The world's first self-transporting fuel will eventually be used to power cars, electricity plants, aeroplanes etc. This will phase out fossil fuel and eliminate the methane which will be consumed by the world's engines. Professor J. J. Lucie of the Farters United For Fuel (FUFF) Institute had this to say about the scheme: 'By the year 2007, we expect the Farts for Fuel operation to be up and running. A critical problem to overcome is getting the size of the gas-bags just right. The first lot we tried were too large and, when filled, caused all the sheep and some of the smaller cows to float off into the sky, endangering air traffic. Another worry is the sheer size of the Fart Zeppelins which must be fault-free: imagine the effect of 5,000,000 concentrated farts being released simultaneously!'

Professor Lucie denied rumours that there were plans to collect human farts for fuel. 'It is theoretically possible for a human to transport himself with his own wind. For instance, a small motorbike could be powered by a tube connected to the rider's bum. However, we have calculated that the cost of the phenomenal quantities of beans required to produce the steady output of farts would be more than the cost of petrol and would therefore not be economical for drivers, if admittedly more environmentally friendly. Mind you, it would add a whole new element to travel sickness!'

THE WINDIEST CITIES IN THE WORLD

THE BLEAUFART SCALE

FORCE	DESCRIPTION	SPECIFICATIONS FOR USE IN VICINITY OF FARTS
0	Calm	Smell rises vertically and usually only affects the farter.
I	Light air	Direction of wind shown by smell drift, which can be most easily observed in a crowd. Watch the faces around a fart to see which way it is headed.
2	Light breeze	Wind felt if standing too close to a farter; light cotton or silk trousers moved by fart.
3	Gentle breeze	Paper on nearby desks in constant motion; wind rises and lifts loose t-shirts slightly.
4	Moderate breeze	Some noise occurs; fart affects all within a 10ft radius.
5	Fresh breeze	May squeal slightly; fart fills small room.
6	Strong breeze	May consist of several parts; whistling heard in trousers; doors to room in which fart is occurring closed with difficulty.
7	Near gale	Whole intestine in motion; inconvenience felt when walking; dangerous in public place.
8	Gale	Expands heavy denim jeans; generally impedes progress; goes on for at least 30 seconds.
9	Hurricane	Lifts small dogs from the ground; causes the evacuation of buildings; leaves trail of devastation in pants.
10	Tornado	Strikes in short, violent bursts; causes concentrated bouts of damage, including holes in clothes, demolition of sheds; lifts turf from bowling greens.

I have been out testing my Fartometer in various parts of the world and sounding out the statistics on where you can go for a really good dose of wind.

City	Country	Bleaufart Rating	Specialities
Kingstonne	Jamaica	10	Soursap juice
Crapetown	South Africa	10	Biltong (spicy, dried, raw meat)
Farto, North Dakota	USA	10	Scrambled eggs on wholewheat toast
Chittagong	Bangladesh	10	Curried lentils & channa dal
Ostende	Belgium	9	Wheat beer
Cork	Ireland	9	Colcannon (cabbage & potato)
Brownsville, Texas	USA	8	Black-eye beans & belly pork
Honofufu, Hawaii	USA	8	Under-ripe exotic fruits
Rennes	France	8	Onion tart; runny cheese
Banff	Canada	7	Elk steak
Fart William	Scotland	7	Haggis, neeps & tatties
Hoota	Azores	7	Smoked fish
Fartu	Byelorussia	6	Borscht (cabbage & beetroot soup)
Chicago, Illinois	USA	6	Bubble gum
Mexico Chity	Mexico	5	Refried beans & chilli
Hofart	Australia	4	Weetbix
Frankfart	Germany	4	Sauerkraut

BIBLIOGRAPHY & FURTHER READING

Benjamin Franklin wrote a book called *Fart Proudly*.
It is hard to find but you might be lucky enough to come across it.

As well as very kindly letting me use his Colonel Gaddhafi story, John Simpson has contacted me to tell me a bit more about Sir Richard Burton, whose story about the farting exploits of Abu Hasan from his translation of *The Book of the Thousand Nights and a Night* was included in my previous book. He was an avid collector of books about all kinds of 'personal' subjects, most of which his wife refused to acknowledge. He once wrote a manuscript entitled 'A History of Farting', which he produced during one of his wife's tea parties in order to shock everyone. However, it is not clear if it was published or if any copies survive until this day.

Wind-surfing: There are many well-stocked fartsites on the Web these days for interested browsers.

You can also order all the following titles, and more, directly from **Michael O'Mara Books**.

The Little Book of Farting	Alec Bromcie	£1.99
The Complete Book of Farting	Alec Bromcie	£4.99
The History of Farting	Dr Benjamin Bart	£4.99
Tail Winds	Peter Furze	£4.99
Thunder, Flush and Thomas Crapper	Adam Hart-Davis	£3.99
The Little Book of Pants	Vestan Pance	£1.99
The Little Book of Pants 2	Vestan Pance	£1.99
The Little Toilet Book	compiled by David Brown	£1.99

Please allow for postage and packing:
UK: free delivery.   Europe: add 20% of retail price.
Rest of World: add 30% of retail price.

95

To order any of the above or any other Michael O'Mara titles, please call our credit card orderline or fill in this coupon and send/fax to:

Michael O'Mara Books, 250 Western Avenue, London W3 6EE, UK

Telephone 020 8324 5652 Facsimile 020 8324 5678

I enclose a UK bank cheque made payable to

MOM Bookshop Ltd for £_____

Please charge £_____ to my Access/Visa/Delta/Switch

Card No. _____

Expiry date: _____   Switch Issue No._____

NAME (Block Letters please):

_____

ADDRESS:

_____

_____

POSTCODE: _____   TELEPHONE: _____

SIGNATURE:_____